SRI HARSHA OF KANAUJ

SRI HARSHA OF KANAUJ

A monograph on the history of India in the first half of the 7th century A.D.

BY

K. M. PANIKKAR, B. A. (OXON.)

GYAN

Published by

GYAN

Gyan Publishing House
5, Ansari Road
Daryaganj, New Delhi-110002
Phone: 011-47034999, 9811692060
E-mail: books@gyanbooks.com

Distribution Network
gyanbooks.com
India, USA, Canada, UK, Australia

ISBN: 978-81-212-7218-6 (HB)
First Published, 1922

2nd Impression 2024

Printed at: Gyan Press, Delhi.

SRI HARSHA OF KANAUJ
Author: K. M. PANIKKAR

SRI HARSHA OF KANAUJ.

A monograph on the history of India in the first half of the 7th century A.D.

BY

K. M. PANIKKAR, B. A. (Oxon.)

(Sometime Research Scholar of Christ Church, Senior Professor of History and Political Science, Member of the Academic Council, Muslim University, Aligarh, and Fellow of the Indian Women's University, Poona.

AUTHOR OF—

The Problems of Greater India.
Educational Reconstruction in India.
Indian Nationalism : Its Principles and History. (London, 1920.)
Imperialism—A Study in European Expansion.

BOMBAY:

D. B. TARAPOREVALA SONS & CO.
190 Hornby Road, Fort.

1922

CONTENTS

Note.

For the chapter dealing with Harsha's literary achievements I have used some material kindly placed at my disposal by Pandit Sastry A. D. Harisarma of Cochin. I am deeply grateful to him for it,

K. M. PANIKKAR.

Chapter I.

THE POLITICAL CONDITION OF INDIA IN THE 6th CENTURY.

The splendid empire of the Guptas was already reduced to a shadow at about the beginning of the 6th century. During the reign of its last great ruler Narasimha Gupta Baladitya, the Huns under a chieftain named Toramana wrested from the empire the province of Malwa where they established for themselves an independent kingdom. These people belonged to a race of barbarian nomadic tribes who had during the previous century occupied Turkistan and established an empire with Herat as its centre. To their onslaught the Gupta empire succumbed, and though a branch of the imperial dynasty continued to flourish in Magadha till about 750 A.C., it no longer exercised any authority except in the immediate vicinity of the capital. With the invasion of Toramana, the imperial Guptas, for all practical purposes, passed out of Indian history.

Toramana founded an independent kingdom in Malwa where he reigned peacefully till about A.D. 510. On his death he was succeeded by Mihirakula whom a learned historian of ancient India has described as the Attila of Indian Huns. There is a singular unanimity of opinion with regard to the character of his reign. It was tyrannical beyond endurance, and in Mihirakula stood exemplified all the savage characteristics of his race. On some slight pretext he issued an order for the ruthless persecution of Buddhist priests. A confederacy of

Indian rulers under Baladitya of Māgadha and Yasodharman of Malwa saved the country from his ravages by inflicting a crushing defeat on him in 528 A.C. Mihirakula was taken prisoner, but his life was spared at the intercession of the mother of Baladitya[1]. Mihirakula sought and found an asylum in Kashmir, for which act of magnanimity this modern Attila repaid his host shortly afterwards by stirring up a rebellion in the country and finally deposing the king himself. Mihirakula, however, did not live long to enjoy his ill-gotten gains and with him ended the short-lived kingdom of the Huns.

From the break-up of the Gupta empire (Circa 500 A.C.) up to the accession of Harsha in 604 the political history of India is that of a period of transition unrelieved either by great names or by great events. Of Yasodharman, the victor of Mihirakula, we know very little except that he was the ruler of an empire even bigger than that of the Guptas[2]. That he did not establish a new imperial dynasty is clear as we see new kingdoms springing up all over Northern India within the next few years of his great victory. The country south of the Vindhyas was consolidated into a powerful empire by the Chalukya king Pulikesin I at about the middle of 6th century and in the extreme south the long-established Pallava power held sway. It would perhaps be useful for us to take a bird's eye view of the new states which thus sprang up in Northern India.

Beal, Vol. I. pp. 167–172.

Mandasor stone inscription, C. I. I. p. 142.

In the kingdom of Māgadha the descendents of the Gupta emperors ruled. The only important thing we know of them is that they were incessantly fighting the Mukhāri kings who were their neighbours. Isani Varman Mukhāri, we are told, was defeated by Kumāra Gupta of Māgadha. His son Damodara Gupta, who carried on the family feud, was killed by the Mukhāri chieftain. The son of this Damodara Gupta, Mahasena Gupta by name, made war on Sustira Varma of Kamarupa, the father of Bhaskara Varma, the friend of Yuan Chwang and the ally of Sri Harsha. The following is the list of the later Guptas of Māgadha as identified by their inscriptions:—

Krishna Gupta
|
Harsha Gupta
|
Jivita Gupta
|
Kumara Gupta
|
Damodara Gupta
|
Mahasena Gupta
|
Madhava Gupta

Next to Māgadha was the kingdom of Karna Suvarna. The ruling family professed Brahmanism and we are told by Yuan Chwang that the followers of the Buddha were persecuted by Karna Suvarna kings. The kingdom of Kámarupa or Assam lay to the east of this country, and here also the prevailing religion was that of the Brahmans. The ruling family was a very ancient one and Yuan Chwang's statement that Bháskara Varman's family had been in possession of the country for thousands of years has been borne out by a copper plate grant of that monarch which has been lately discovered at Nidhanpur[1]. The last four names mentioned in that grant are also mentioned in Bāna's *Harsha Charita*. Bhagadatta, from whom the Kámarupa family traced its descent, was an important personality even in the time of the Mahabharata, and from that mythological personage we have in historical times a long line of kings—a fact which goes to prove that the independence of that mountainous country had been well-preserved during all the turmoils that overtook the Gangetic plain. Yasodharman is the only monarch who is definitely[2] mentioned to have conquered Kámarupa, for his empire is said to have extended to the banks of the Brahmaputra[3]. Of the important position that Kámarupa under Bhaskara Varman occupied as an ally of Harsha we shall have to allude to later on.

On the south-western border of Aryavarta a new and powerful dynasty was established in the 6th century by Sĕnăpthi Bhattaraka. The Maliya copper plate inscription of Maharajah Dhruvasena II dated A.D.[4] 571

---

[1] Indian Antiquary, May, 1914, P. Bhattacharya.

[2] Mandasor stone inscription, Corpus Inscriptionis Indicarum (C. I. I.) p. 142.

[3] आलौहि त्येपकण्ठा.

[4] C. I. I. p. 164,

tells us that Sĕnăpati Bhattaraka acquired great glory in a hundredth battle fought against the Maihatas. Taking great advantage of the state of anarchy following the fall of the Gupta Empire, this adventurous general carved out a kingdom for himself. He was succeeded by his son Sēnāpati Dharmasena whose brother, Drona Sinha, assumed the style and title of Maharaja and was probably recognised as such by other kings. During the 6th century this family aggrandised itself so much at the expense of its neighbours that a collateral branch came to be established in Malwa. The Vallabhi kings were Saivaites by religion with the exception of Dharapatta, a most devout worshipper of the sun.

Of Malwa itself we know nothing after the meteoric appearance of Yasodharman. Who this Yasodharman was, how long he reigned, we cannot say. He seems to have sprung up from nowhere, and disappeared into nothingness after breaking up the kingdom of the Huns and establishing for himself an empire greater in extent, than that of the Guptas.

Thus Northern India had again become divided into a number of minor principalities whose political history is merely a record of dynastic wars. But it would be a mistake to infer from this that India in the 6th century had relapsed into anarchy. What had happened was that the strong disruptive forces, which even the imperial tradition of the Mauryas and the Guptas had not been able to eradicate, asserted themselves again for a short time as a result of the Hun invasions. The great movements which started in the time of the Guptas continued to progress. The revival of Sanskrit, associated as it is with the evolution of Neo-Hinduism and the absorption by it of Mahāyāna Buddhism, was fast approaching culmination. The great intellectual activity which manifested itself under the Guptas in the 5th century did not decline with the disappearance of the Empire. Varaha Mihira, the astronomer, Arya Bhatta, the mathematician, and many others less known to fame illumined the comparative political darkness of the 6th century.

The gradual re-assertion of Brahminical religion in a new garb is, without doubt, the characteristic feature of the 6th century. A comparison between the descriptions of Fa-Hien who visited India in the 5th century, and of Yuan Chwang who resided for some time at the court of Harsha in the middle of the first half of the 7th century, will clearly prove the great change that had taken place in the religious history of India during the 6th century. When Fa Hien visited the country, the Dharma was still predominant in Aryavarta in spite of the official patronage of Brahminism by the imperial family. The country was full of richly endowed Sangharamas where learning and religion flourished. In Muttra alone the pious pilgrim found not less than 20 monasteries inhabited by more than 3,000 monks who tried to follow the Noble Eighth-fold Path of the Enlightened One. Wherever the pilgrim went he found that the Buddhist monks were held in high respect and Buddhist learning cultivated. Within a century and a half this state of affairs was completely changed. In a later chapter we shall attempt to discuss at some length the reasons for so great a change. For our present purpose it is sufficient to recognise that in spite of the patronage of the great emperor Harsha himself the position of Buddhism when Yuan Chwang visited India had been completely undermined. Brahminism had within a century and a half gained considerable ground at the expense of its rival.

The 6th century witnessed this geat religious transformation. What had happened was, in fact, merely the reassertion of the great genius of Hinduism. It should never be forgotten that Buddhism was, to start with, nothing more than one of the numerous reforming sects of Hinduism and such it continued to be till the humane Piya dasi gave it his imperial patronage. When Asoka died after a long life of enthusiastic missionary work Buddhism had developed its distinct characteristics as against the older faith. But a process of approximation soon began to take place again. The more Buddhism became the dominant religious faith of India, the closer became the approximation between the great mass of popular traditions which went by the name of *Arya Dharma* and the tenets of the noble creed preached by Gautama. The question finally became merely one of priesthood, *i.e.*, whether the yellow-robed monks of Buddhism or the orthodox Brahmins were to have the dominant influence with kings and princes. As the Gupta emperors were Brahminically inclined without however any pronounced hostility towards the followers of the other creed, the displacement of the yellow robe had begun, even when the pious Fa Hien was diligently taking down the traditions in various Buddhist monasteries.

In India thus the 6th century after Christ was essentially a period of transition. It may with sufficient accuracy be characterised as an age of preparation when the forces of historical growth were working imperceptibly towards a mighty religious transformation. The political unity of India also was broken up during this period into many principalities, affording ample field for another Chandra Gupta to weld them into a single national state. It is only the next century that witnessed the full working out of these tendencies, as we shall attempt to show in the following pages.

Chapter II.

THE POLITICAL HISTORY OF THE REIGN OF HARSHA.

Of Harsha's ancestry not much is known. Even his poetic biographer Bāna, unable to connect his hero with either of the two mythological progenitors of Indian royal families, the sun and the moon, contents himself by saying that "there arose a monarch named Pushpabhuti, framed as it were with the compound splendour of all primæval kings[1] from whom was descended a long line of illustrious monarchs." Bāna, however, does not mention the name of any of them till we come down to Prabhakara Vardhana, (surnamed 'the mighty' Pratāpa Sīla) the father of Harsha. By the patient researches of modern scholars, we are now able to trace Harsha's ancestors to three generations before Prabhakara Vardhana. The Sonpat copper seal[2] of Harsha Vardhana, himself mentions Sri Rajya Vardhana as the grandfather of Prabhakara. Rajya Vardhana's son and successor was Aditya Vardhana who married a princess by the name Mahasena Gupta Devi. Their son was Prabhakara Vardhana, known to his contemporaries as the valiant victor of the Huns and to history as the father of one of India's greatest monarchs.

Prabhakara's ancestors were no more than petty Rajahs holding sway over the districts that surrounded

---

[1] Bana's Harsha Carita, published by the R. A. S. of London, translated by Cowell & Thomas, p. 83.

[2] Corpus Inscriptionis Indicarum. Vol. III. (C. I. I.) Fleet's Gupta inscriptions, p. 231 et seq.

Thaneswar. They were devout worshippers of the sun.[1] They do not seem to have been prominent in the politics of North India during the days of anarchy resulting from the break-up of the Gupta Empire. It was Prabhakara Vardhana that first assumed the title of Maharajadhiraja, his predecessors having been content with the humbler one of Maharaja. It is clear from the descriptions of Bāna that Prabhakara Vardhana repulsed more than once the predatory invasions of the Huns, with whom as the ruler of a March he came often in contact. He also subdued Malwa and at least attacked, if he did not conquer, even the distant state of Gujarat. By these and other warlike operations he achieved fame for himself and laid the foundations of an empire, the superstructure of which his greater son was destined to raise.

Prabhakara Vardhana married Yasōvati by whom he had two sons and a daughter. Harsha was the second son, his elder brother being named Rajya Vardhana. Rajya Sri, their only sister, was nearly 2 years' younger than Harsha.

Harsha was born "in the month of Jaishta on the 12th day of the dark fortnight (Krishna paksha) the pleiads being in the ascendant, just after the twilight time."[2] His brother was five years senior to him. The boys had as their playmate their cousin Bandi, the son of

---

1 Sonpat seal: C. I. I. Vol III. p. 231. 2 Cowell Thomas. Translation of Bana's Harshacharita (C. & T.) p. 109.

Yasovati's brother, who was almost of the same age as Rajya Vardhana. The king also selected as fit companions for the princes the two sons of the conquered king of Malwa, Kumara Gupta and Madhava Gupta by names, who had been evidently brought up under the care of Prabhakara Vardhana himself. These young men had been "found by frequent trials untouched by any taint of vice, blameless, discreet, strong and comely." [1]

The princess Rajya Sri was married when she grew up to be a girl of 12 or 13 years of age to Grahavarman, the son of Avanta Varman Mukhari. The Mukharis were a most illustrious family[1] but they do not seem to have attained great political power at any time. They were related by marriage to most of the important royal families of North India and we know them from inscriptions as carrying on an unceasing family feud[1] against the Guptas of Magadha.

As the princes Rajya Vardhana and Harsha grew up the king associated them more and more with his government. In the Hindu system of polity the Yuvaraja has a distinct position and he shares with his father the responsibilities of State affairs. Thus when Rajya Vardhana was old enough for wearing armour the king placed him at the head of an immense force and sent him attended by ancient advisers and devoted feudatories

---

1 Apsad stone inscription of Adityasena, C. I. I.

towards the North to attack the Huns. Harsha was also sent with him. When the princes were thus absent from the capital Prabhakara Vardhana fell seriously ill Harsha, who was too young to join the campaign, though he had accompanied the army, at once returned to attend his father on his death-bed. Before the Yuva-raja Rajya Vardhana could return from the front the old king was dead. Queen Yasōvati chose to die on the funeral pyre of her lord and Harsha undertook the government of the realm till the return of his brother.

Rajya Vardhana did not abandon the field of war in order to hasten to the capital where he knew the administration will be conducted in his name by Harsha. When the war was over and the victorious Rajya Vardhana was back in his own he found that a new campaign awaited him. News was brought to him almost immediately on his return that his brother-in-law, Graha Varman Mukhari, had been foully murdered by the king of Malwa and his sister Rajya Sri cast into prison at Kanyakubja "like a brigand's wife with a pair of iron fetters kissing her feet."[1] The Rajah of Malwa had perhaps considered the death of Prabhakara Vardhana and the absence of Rajya Vardhana on his campaign against the Huns as a suitable opportunity to reassert his independence. Rajya Vardhana accompanied by his minister Bandi immediately set out to punish the rebel vassal who had insulted the race of

1 C. & T. p. 178.

Pushpabhuti. Harsha, in spite of his protests and entreaties, was left behind at the capital.

Rajya Vardhana defeated the rebellious king of Malwa and took full revenge on him. But the Gauda king of Karna Suvarna[1] Sasanka by name, who was perhaps an ally of the enemy, enticed him by false civilities and murdered him.[2] As Harsha was not grown up to mature age and as Rajya Vardhana's children, if he had any, were still in their swaddling clothes, it was perhaps the expectation of the rebels that, at least after the death of Rajya Vardhana, the kingdom of Thaneswar would be left without proper government, at the tender mercy of every adventurer with a strong arm. A better motive could perhaps be found in the fact that Rajya Vardhana, after defeating the Malwa king, attempted to extend his territory eastward and conquer the king of Karna Suvarna who finding himself unable to meet the Rajah of Thaneswar in open field foully murdered him after making a show of submission. Inscriptions tell us that the "Paramabhattaraka Maharajadhiraja Sri Rajya Vardhana......... after defeating in battle a confederacy of princes under Deva Guptas undertook the conquest of the world."[3] Whatever be the motive, whether it be the break-up of the Thaneswar kingdom or the preservation of local independence, the expectations of the rebels were soon falsified. The elders of the

1 Beal. Chinese Knowledge of the Western World. Trubner's Classics, Vol. I. p. 210. 2 C. & T., p. 208. 3 Epigraphia Indica, Vol. VII. p. 185.

kingdom led by Senapati Simhanada[1] at once proclaimed Harsha king.

For some reason which is not quite plain, Harsha was reluctant to accept the Crown. Both Bāna and Yuan Chwang agree that it was only after considerable hesitation that Harsha was persuaded upon to accept the Crown. Yuan Chwang tells us a story of Harsha, rent asunder by conflicting feelings of religiousness and worldliness, having recourse to a Boddhisatwa in order to seek his advice. That wise man according to the Chinese pilgrim advised Harsha not to ascend the Simhāsana, or the lion throne, or take the title of king but to rule with all the authority of royalty.[2] Mr. Vincent Smith explains the reluctance of Harsha by suggesting that he had early in his life accepted the yellow robe or at least become attached as a lay brother. There is nothing to prove or disprove this hypothesis. But we must remember that Harsha himself definitely tended to the Buddhist doctrine only after Yuan Chwang's visit, and hence it is quite improbable that he had joined the Order either as a monk or as a lay brother in his early life. The young prince's reluctance may have been due merely to the recognition of the fact

---

1 Mr. Vincent Smith and others say that it was on the proposal of Bhandin, the cousin of the late king, that Harsha was elected. This is hardly possible as Bhandin had accompanied the king in his Malwa campaign. C. & T., p. 254. The mistake possibly arose out of Yuan Chwang's statement that Bani was the one who proposed.

2 Beal, Vol. I. p. 213.

that the inheritance which he was called upon to succeed to, was not a particularly comfortable one especially as the feudatories had shown themselves refractory and rebellious. It may also be that his brother Rajya Vardhana had left an heir to the kingdom, in which case Harsha might have properly enough felt scruples about disinheriting him. But if the arguments of the State Council and the advice of Avanti, the foreign minister, were not sufficient to set aside these scruples, whatever they may have been due to, the convenient appearance of the Goddess of Royal Prosperity[1] according to Bāna, or the counsels of a Buddhist sage according to Yuan Chwang, persuaded Harsha that a great and noble future was awaiting him as the emperor of Hindustan.

As soon as Harsha had taken over the administration he vowed that he will not rest till he had avenged the murder of his brother and the ill-treatment of his sister. Harsha's immediate objects were two: He wanted to take Kanyakubja and set free his sister who was imprisoned there, and he wanted to punish Sasānka, the king of Karna Suvarna. On his way he was met by an envoy of Bhaskara Varman, the Kumara Rajah of Kamarupa. Bhaskara was the younger son of Sustira Varman. His elder brother Suprathistita Varman being the ruler, Bhaskara is generally spoken of by Yuan Chwang as Kumara. Whether it was for the purpose of displacing his brother with the help of a powerful friend or merely because the ruler of Karna Suvarna was their common

---

C. & T., p. 78.

enemy, Bhaskara Varman offered his alliance to Harsha. For Harsha the proposed alliance should certainly have been welcome as it made the conquest of Karna Suvarna, which was bounded on the eastern side by Kamarupa, an easy matter. Bhaskara seems to have been an ambitious and enlightened prince who thoroughly appreciated the value of Harsha's friendship and the alliance between the two continued unbroken as we shall see, to the very end.

After concluding this welcome alliance Harsha marched on against Sasanka when his cousin Bhandi, who had accompanied Rajya Vardhana in his Malwa campaign, arrived in camp with prisoners and booty.[1] Bhandi also gave him news of his sister about whom he was most anxious. He was told that the princess, as soon as she had heard about the death of Rajya Vardhana, fearing humiliation or worse at the hands of Narendra Gupta, who had occupied Kanyakubja, had fled to the Vindhya hills. Harsha immediately set out to seek her, leaving Bhandi as the commander of the troops against Sasanka. With the help of Nirghuta, the nephew of Bnir Kampa, a chief of the hill tribes in the locality, Harsha searched all the Vindhyas and was enabled finally to rescue Rajya Sri when at the point of committing suicide. The rescued princess asked to be allowed to take the red robe saying it was immodesty for a woman who had lost her husband even to continue to live as a fuel for misery. Harsha probably consented to this for we are told that he

---

1 C. & T., p. 254.

employed a renowned Buddhist sage to discourse to her on the Noble Eighthfold Path.

As to how Bhandi fared in his campaign against Sasanka we are not expressly told. But it seems probable that Gauda king accepted Harsha's suzerainty and was allowed by him to rule his state as a vassal. A mound at Rohtasgadh[1] describes him as a Mahāsāmanta or vassal Rajah. Later on, however, he seems to have revolted, as an inscription dated 619 A.C. has been discovered, in which he describes himself as Maharajadhiraja Sasanka.[2] But the revolt was short-lived and Karna Suvarna was finally reduced, part of it being annexed to Harsha's empire and part to Bhaskara's kingdom of Kāmarupa. It seems that Harsha received valuable help from his ally in this as the Nidhanpur copper-plate of Bhaskara[3] shows that at least the eastern portion of Karna Suvarna was definitely annexed to Kāmarupa. The reduction of this kingdom must have brought the whole of Northern India under Harsha's sway. Malwa had already been conquered by Rajya Vardhana and on the North-West the Huns had been defeated and driven back even in the time of Prabhakara Vardhana. In fact, Harsha's Northern Indian Empire was not entirely built up by him. The campaigns of the mighty Prabhakara Vardhana had laid the foundations on which it was built.

---

[1] C. I. I, Vol, III. p. 283. [2] Epigraphia Indica, Vol. VI, p. 143. [3] Indian Antiquary, 1914.

Within 6 years after his accession the young king was the supreme lord, Paramēswara, of Northern India. As to whether Harsha invaded and conquered Nepal there is still considerable difference of opinion among scholars.[1] The facts with regard to subject are the following: An inscription, dated Sri Harsha Samvat 34 by the Nepalese Rajah Amsu Varman, has been discovered 4 miles to the south of Katmandu.[2] We are told by Yuan Chwang that "lately there was a king called Amsu Varman in Nepal who had written a book on Sabda Vidya."[3] The Vamsavali, or the Chronicles of Nepal, informs us that before the accession of Amsu Varman, Vikramaditya invaded Nepal and established his era there.[4] More than all this we have a Statement in *Harsha Charita* which implies that Harsha conquered an Himalayan territory difficult of access. Against this almost conclusive mass of evidence we have to place two minor points which militate against our inference. One is that the Nepalese Vamsavali mentions only one Amsu Varman and he is stated in it to have been crowned in Kali Era 3000–101 B.C. The evidence of Vamsavali in

---

1 The following are the chief contributions to this discussion:—

Sylvain Levi, Nepal une Royaume Hindou.
Indian Antiquary, Vol. XIII, p. 413.
Keilhorn List of N. Inscriptions.
Epigraphica Indica, Vol. v. app. p. 75.
Buhler's Essays on Inscriptions, Nepal (1885)

2. No. 6 insc. from Nepal. (Dr. Indraji). 3 Beal, Vol. II, p. 81.
4. Wright's Nepal p. 131.

the matter of chronology is of no importance especially as we have the authority of Yuan Chwang himself that Amsu Varman was almost contemporaneous to him. The second point is much more serious. Yuan Chwang's statement that "lately there was a king named Amsu Varman" seems to imply that he had recently died when the Chinese pilgrim was travelling in India. It has been established beyond any possibility of doubt that Yuan Chwang was in India between 637 and 642. If Amsu Varman was dead at that time he could not possibly have dated the Katmandu inscription previously alluded to in year 34 or Sri Harsha Samvat. We know that Harsha came to the throne at about 606 (the earliest possible date) and hence the 34th year of Harsha Samvat would mean 640 A.C. If we are to accept Yuan Chwang's statement this would clearly be impossible. But we must remember that the Chinese pilgrim does not say that he visited Nepal. In his life there is no mention of any place between Vetapur and Magadha. Under these conditions it is possible that Yuan was not correctly informed with regard to his death.

However, two facts are established indisputably. (1) A Rajah named Amsu Varman ruled in Nepal in the beginning of the 7th century and (2) he used an Indian era which was only recently instituted. As we know that eras are established only by king's claiming to be sovereign of the whole of Arya Varta there is no other era but Harsha's possibly in the beginning of the 7th century. There is another reason which clearly proves that the era used in the Nepal inscriptions was that of Harsha. Nepal inscriptions Nos. 12 and 13 by Siva Deva are dated 119 and 113 Samvat. We are told in the inscription of Jaya Deva (153) that Siva Sena married the grand-daughter of Aditya Sēna. Aditya Sēna's date can easily be fixed from his Apshad stone inscription[1] which says that his father Mahasena Gupta was the contemporary and friend of Harsha. The Shahpur stone image inscription of Adityasena is dated 672 A.C. His grand-daughter Vatsadevi was married to Siva Gupta of Nepal, and if we take 50 years as a possible distance between his reign and the youth of his grand-daughter we can place the reign of Siva Deva in 720 A.C. onwards. The first inscription of Siva Deva is placed 119 Samvat, and dating it from Harsha's accession in 606, we have it as 725 A.C. These facts clearly show that Harsha Era was used in Nepal and that Harsha's supremacy was recognized even in that distant and inaccessible kingdom.

It must have been after his conquest of North India that Harsha changed the capital of his State from Thaneswar to Kanyakubja, or the modern Kanauj. Kanyakubja was at that time an important city with a tradition of civic life. We are told by Yuan Chwang that it was 20 *li* in length and about 5 or 6 *li* in breadth. On the western side it was bordered by the Ganges; on the other three sides it had a dry ditch with strong and lofty towers facing one another. That it was a no mean

---

1 C. I. I.

city even when Harsha selected it for capital is quite evident from the fact that Ptolemy makes mention of it [1] and Fa-Hien tells us of two Sanghāramas both belonging to the HīnaYána sect which existed there in his time. [2] Near there the Buddha is reported to have preached to his disciples on Impermanency and Sorrow. Though great in this way even before the 7th century, Kanauj must have rivalled the glories of Pataliputra of the Mauryas and Ujjain of the Guptas, when it became the capital of Harsha. Yuan Chwang tells us that there were some hundreds of Sanghāramas and about 200 Hindu temples when he visited the place. In India it has been the custom from time immemorial for powerful emperors from Yudhistira to Akbar to found new cities or renovate old ones in order to equal the legendary capitals of previous monarchs. The magnificent ruins at Fatehpur Sikri still attest to this great tendency of Indian monarchs. Harsha, we may be sure, spared no efforts to make Kanauj worthy to be compared to the most renowned cities of old. It remained the most important city in North India long after his death for we find that it was in a most flourishing condition even at the time of Mohammed Ghori's invasion in the 12th century.

The change of capital was due to no mere caprice. Harsha's own ancestral capital of Thaneswar was merely the chief city of a small kingdom. With the expansion

[1] Lib. 7. I. 22. [2] Beal.

of his empire to the borders of Assam and the establishment of his suzerainty all over North India it became necessary for him to have a more central capital from which he could exercise his authority all over his vast dominions. Moreover, the position of Thaneswar was such that it was open to attack from the North-West. Though for the time the Huns had been driven out of the borders of India, they were so firmly established on the Frontier that an exposed capital like Thaneswar was certainly a matter of danger. Harsha may have therefore thought it more prudent to shift his capital to a more central place.

Harsha seems to have brought the whole of Northern India under his control. But this, however, did not satisfy him. Like Samudra Gupta his ambition was to be the lord of the entire Bhárata Varsha. With this object he led an army into the Deccan. He was not, however, destined to repeat the exploits of Samudra Gupta, for on reaching the Narbada he found his career of victory arrested by the opposition of a foreman worthy of his steel. This was Pulikesin II. of the Chálukyas. The Chalukyan Empire, which Pulikesin I. founded in the middle of the 6th century, had united the tribes of the Mahratta country into a mighty state.[1] Pulikesin I. had considered himself great enough to celebrate a horse sacrifice. His son, Kirti Varman, extended his father's conquest and we are told in the inscription of Mahákuta that he conquered Anga, Vanga, Magadha and other

---

1 Indian Antiquary, Vol. III, p. 305,

kingdoms.[1] Kirti Varman, we know from the Chiplun plates, [2] married a daughter of Sēnānanda Raja, but seems to have died when his son was not old enough to assume the reins of government. Mangalēsa, the brother of the dead king, usurped the throne, and we are told euphemistically that Kīrti Varman's son, Pulikesin, framed a resolution to wander abroad as an exile. But on Mangalēsa's death in 609 A.C. Pulikesin seems to have returned and taken possession of his father's realm without opposition.

Pulikesin II. inherited from his uncle a consolidated kingdom which extended from the Vindhyas to the borders of the Pallava kingdom in the south. He seems to have extended it further. From his Aihole inscription dated 634 A.C. we learn that he subdued the Malwas, the Gurjaras and the Kalingas.[3] It was this powerful monarch who stood in the way of Harsha's attempted conquest of the south. As to when this encounter took place we cannot exactly say. Mr. Vincent Smith in his ***Early History***[4] says that it took place in 620 A.C. This is certainly incorrect as the Aihole inscription (634 A.C.) which recounts the achievement of Pulikesin does not mention what is without doubt the greatest victory of the reign and of which Pulikesin was naturally enough very proud. Allusions to the encounter with

---

1. Indian Antiquary, Vol. XIX, P. 7.
2. Ep. Ind., Vol. III, p. 51.
3. Aihole inscription. Epigraphica Indica, Vol. VI, p. 4.
4. E. H. I, p. 340, 3rd edition.

Harsha are very frequent in the inscriptions dated after 636 and Pulikesin is spoken of from that time as "Harsha Vichēda hetu" or the conqueror of Harsha. He is also spoken of as one who by the fear caused to be broken the joy of Harsha (Bhaya visalita harsho yēna cākari Harsha). It is clear that Pulikesin would not omit to mention this great achievement of his in an inscription where he boasted of lesser conquests.[1] It seems therefore clear that the date of Harsha's invasion of the south and his defeat at the hands of Pulikesin II. took place in 636 A.C. and not as Mr. Vincent Smith states in 620.

This is all the more probable since we know that Harsha attacked and defeated Dhruva Sena the Vallabhi king in 636. This king was, according to Yuan Chwang, a man of hasty temper and shallow views but a sincere believer in Buddhism. Harsha led an expedition against him and Dhruva Sena (or Dhruva Bhatta) was defeated and his country conquered. The defeated king fled to Dadda IV. of Broach.[2] Partly through the intervention of that king and partly because Harsha wanted to safeguard his line of communication in his campaign against the Chalukya monarch the Vallabhi king was generously treated. He was reinstated on the throne of his fathers and Harsha gave him his daughter in marriage. It was after this that Harsha attacked Pulikesin. But the Goddess of Royal Prosperity who promised him protection at the beginning of his reign

---

1 Aihole inscription. 2 Indian Antiquary, Vol. XIII.

does not seem to have showered her blessings on him on this occasion. The emperor of the North was arrested in his career of victory and Harsha, like a wise monarch, did not persist in his attempts but merely retreated to his capital leaving the frontier in charge of his son-in-law Dhruva Sena (or Dhruva Bhatta) of Vallabhi.

Pulikesin did not live very long after this victory. His fame as a mighty king spread far and wide and he entered into diplomatic relations with the king of Persia. The Arab historian Tabani tells us that in the 36th year of the reign of Khusru II. (*i.e.*, 626 A.C.) Parameswara, king of India, sent to the Persian Court an embassy with a letter of greeting.[1] A fresco painting in the caves of Ajanta represents the reception of a Persian embassy at the Chalukya Court and another painting represents Khusru drinking wine with his favourite queen. All the evidence, we have, goes to prove that Pulikesin was a very powerful monarch who shared with Harsha the sovereignty of India in the first half of the 7th century. Of the date of his death we have no accurate knowledge, but it seems that the revival of Pallava power under Nara Simha Varman Mahamalla—the greatest of that dynasty—administered a check to the Chalukya hegemony of the Deccan.[2] Under Nara Simha Varman the Pallavas marched into the very heart of the Chalukya country and Badami itself was completely destroyed in 640.

---

1 Noeldeke. Gesichichte. Tabri, p. 371.

2 The origin of the Pallava family is obscure. But their sway was unquestioned in the southern country till the rise of the Cholas.

After the arrest of his victorious march Harsha seems to have led a peaceful and quiet life. The whole of Aryavarta accepted him as lord and master and the country enjoyed peace and good government under his unceasing vigilance. He entered into diplomatic relations with the emperor of China, of whom he had heard from the Chinese pilgrim Yuan Chwang. In 641 A.C.[1] Harsha sent a mission to China and the compliment was returned by the Son of Heaven and friendly relations came to be established between the two empires.

Of the later period of Harsha's life we have no definite knowledge. Our chief authorities, Bāna and Yuan Chwang, break off before this. We know, however, that his religious attitude changed considerably during this time. This was probably due to the influence that the learned Doctor of Laws, Yuan Chwang, gained over his imperial patron. He also celebrated a great religious festival for which all the vassal princes, his faithful ally the Kumara Raja of Kamarupa, and his son-in-law Dhruva Sena of Vallabhi, were invited. Though the position of honour belonged to the great image of the Buddha it was in no sense an exclusively Buddhist carnival, and the principal deities of the Brahmanic pantheon were also honoured. The vivid description that Yuan Chwang gives us, serves to give a clear idea as to the essentially eclectic character of Harsha's religous feeling and his great love for pageantry. We are told that the image of the Buddha was carried in

1 Journal Asiatique, IV Series, Vol. IX, p. 81 et. sqq.

solemn procession with 20 kings, 800 elephants and an immense concourse following it.

An attempt was made by some fanatical Brahmins on this occasion to assassinate the emperor whose pronounced Buddhist sympathies and public patronage of Sramanas must have been looked upon with jealousy and intolerance by them. At this time, it should be remembered, that Brahminism had become an aggressive creed again, thanks to the powerful patronage of the Guptas in the 5th century and the great revival of Sanskrit. Harsha's close association with Buddhism must have made him unpopular with the more bigoted section of the Brahmins, but we have no mention of any further attempt made to assassinate him.

Harsha died in 647 A.C. His empire extended at his death from Kāmarupa on the east to Kashmir on the west, with the Himalayas as the northern and Vindhyas as the southern boundary. The kingdom of Nepal had accepted him as suzerain while in the south the lord of Vallabhi was his vassal and son-in-law. Only against the Chalukyan monarch had his arms failed but the great Pulikesin II himself had died in 642 and his capital Badami had been sacked and destroyed by Mahamalla Pallava. In his later days Harsha was peace-loving, though his peace was based on a large and efficient army. That he did not take advantage of the fall of the Chalukya power is sufficient evidence to the hold which the pacific religion of the Enlightened One came to have on him. But though peace-loving he maintained his hold unshaken on Arya Varta till the end of his days and the closing years of his life were marked by many acts of piety and charity.

Harsha seems to have been unmarried, and in any case it is certain that he left no issue behind him. After his death the country was plunged into anarchy again from which it was destined never entirely to recover till the invasion and conquest of India by the followers of the Arabian Prophet.

CHAPTER III.

HARSHA THE KING.

THE short account given in the previous chapter proves indubitably that Harsha was the greatest monarch of his time in India. He is justly accorded a place in the list of the Great Kings who have ruled over the land of Hindustan from Chandra Gupta to Aurangzeb. The main characteristics of his reign are therefore worth a close study in order to determine his position in Indian history.

There was a distinct and in some ways a very enlightened conception of kingly duties among the Hindus. The Mahabharata—that encyclopædia of Hindu folklore and ethics—discusses elaborately the duties of kings,[1] and the science of politics, known as Artha Sastra, or Rája Niti, which was a highly cultivated branch of knowledge in India, developed an advanced theory of monarchy. No ordinary ruler would have dared and no conscientious one would have liked to infringe so strong a tradition which had the full weight of religious orthodoxy behind it. The ideal of kingship which the Nītī Sashtrās developed was a very high one, and Kautilya, the great minister of Chandra Gupta Maurya and the Machiavelli of the ancient India, himself says that the king's first duty should be the promotion of the happiness of his subjects as therein lies his own happiness.[2] "The ruler, says Sukracharya,

---

1 Rájadharma Sasana Parva. Sect. LXIX.

2 Artha Sastra, Duties of a King, Chapt. XIX.

has been made by Brahma the servant of the people getting his revenue as his remuneration: his sovereignty is only for protection".[1] These high ideals were consciously pursued by many kings whose names shed lustre on the pages of Indian history. "Work I must," said the greatest of Indian monarchs,[4] for public benefit."

These high traditions Harsha also strove to maintain. He was constantly touring his vast dominions with a view to be fully enlightened as to the true condition of his subjects and to remedy their grievances. He gave his personal attention to all matters of importance though following the great Aryan tradition, the administration of the country was left in the hands of a State Council. That the State Council was a permanent feature of Indian polity we know from all the discovered books dealing with statecraft. We also know that it was held in high esteem as an organ of political life. The Lord Buddha when asked by his disciple Ānanda about the prosperity of Vajjiyans told him "Have you heard the Vajjiyans hold full and frequent assemblies?" "Lord, so I have heard," replied he (Ananda). "So long, Ananda," replied the Blessed One, "as the Vajjiyans hold full and frequent assemblies, so long may they be expected not to decline but to prosper"[2]. "The monarch who follows his own will," says Sukra, "is the

---

[1] Sukraniti, p. 71.

[2] Mahāparinibbana Nittanta (Rhys Davids) p. 14.

cause of miseries, soon gets estranged from his kingdom and alienated with his subjects."[1]

How far Harsha's Council was able to control state policy we have no means of knowing. But from the descriptions which we have in Yuan Chwang and Bāna of the authority, that the council exercised at the death of Rajya Vardhana we shall not be greatly mistaken in thinking that it had real power vested in its hands. As to the number of members which the council had both of our authorities are silent. But it is probable that here also the ancient Hindu tradition as described in the Niti Sastras was closely followed. Kautilya lays down the rule, or more correctly the tradition, that the king should be helped by a privy council consisting of the heads of departments. Sukra Niti tells us[2] that the king should have 10 ministers. Of Harsha's council itself we have a passing glimpse. Bāna says that Senapati Simhanada, the foreign minister [3] Avanti, and the keeper of the elephants[4] Skanda Gupta, made speeches advising the prince as to the course he should follow at the crisis of his brother's death.

Thus in times of crisis the council was a body with great authority. Even during the lifetime of the

---

1 Sukraniti, Chap II. p. 55. 2 Ibid Chap. II, slokas 141–48.

3 Samdhi Vigrahadhikula (the one authorised to make war and peace).

4 The keeper of the elephants was as important an official in older days as the civil lord of the admiralty is in modern England.

monarch, the council must have wielded great powers in matters of administration because the king was often touring the country. Thus there can bo no doubt that though Harsha's government was personal in one sense the royal authority was by no means despotic. The reason for this is twofold. First, the existence of local rajahs or sāmantas, who were left more or less in the full enjoyment of their authority, was a great check on royal autocracy. An oppressive ruler like Mihirakula found himself faced by a confederacy of sāmantas. Secondly, the Council of State possessed considerable powers against which it was impossible for any monarch to go.

The government of a large country has always to be a bureaucracy. Administration can only be carried on by a body of officials and in Harsha's empire a highly organised bureaucracy seems to have been in existence. The chief official of the king was the Maha Samdhi Vigrahadhi Kara or the Lord High Chancellor. This office is specifically mentioned by Bāna and we come across it in many inscriptions before and after the time of Harsha. Mahabaladhikrita is mentioned as a great office in supreme command of the Army. Mahakshapatalika[1] or the Lord High Keeper of Records was the functionary in charge of legal documents. The Chamberlains or Mahapratiharas were also officials of great influence. The provinces were governed by Raja Sthāniyas or Viceroys or Kumara Maliyas or

[1] C. I. I., Vol. III, p. 190.

Governors. The chief authority in a city was a Drangika or a Mayor. What his authority was and how it was exercised we do not know. But the mention of Mahattaras—literally greater men— seems to show that some sort of a municipal government existed.

That Harsha's rule was mild and benevolent we are informed by Yuan Chwang. Local Rajahs were allowed to exercise authority subject to an annual tribute and personal attendance at court on ceremonial occasions. We are told by Yuan Chwang that in the great religious assembly convoked in his honour not less than 18 tributary Rajahs, besides the Rajah of Vallabhi and the Kumara Rajah of Kamarupa were present.

Harsha, though he became pacific in his policy towards the end, maintained a large and fully equipped army. Yuan Chwang tells that his military establishment consisted of 5,000 elephants, 20,000 cavalry and 50,000 infantry. That such a standing army required great organisation is clear and from the fact that with it Harsha conquered the whole of North India we may infer that he kept it up in a high state of efficiency. The ideal of Imperial States is certainly not to keep in peace with their neighbours and in India as elsewhere it was considered the duty of the king to keep himself always ready for war as much for defence as for offence. The remarkable thing about Harsha's military establishment is its comparative smallness. Hindu kings, we know, were accustomed to keep huge and unmanageable forces. The Maurya army, we are told, consisted of 30,000 cavalry, 9,000 elephants and 600,000 infantry.[1] The army of the great Vijayanagar kings of the 16th century contained 703,000 infantry, 32,000 horse and 551 elephants and innumerable camp followers.[2] It speaks much for the pacific character of Harsha and the effectiveness of his government that the army he maintained was so small comparatively. That the last 10 years of his reign was spent in peace without having had to meet internal rebellion or external agression shows that his army, though relatively small, was an effective and powerful fighting force.

Harsha's statecraft was thus based on an efficient army. But the army is merely the arm of policy. He secured his frontiers by alliances and marriages. On his eastern boundary he maintained very friendly relations all during his reign with the Kumara Raja of Kamarupa ; and on the south-west where his territory touched that of his mighty rival, Pulikesin, he reinstated the Vallabhi king binding him by the closest ties to the imperial throne. He even maintained friendly relations with the emperor of China, probably as a counterpoise to the friendship that Pulikesin cultivated with the king of Persia.

One other main features of Harsha's rule was his toleration of religious differences. The generous vague-

---

1 Vincent Smith,Early History of India, 3rd. ed., p. 118.
2 Sewell, A Forgotten Empire, p. 147.

ness of Hindu religion allowed room for every sort of opinion and hence dogmatic intolerance and sectarian persecution never very much disgraced Hindu history. Even Asoka, the great missionary of Buddhism, devoted a special edict (No. 12 of Rock Series) to impress upon his subject the supreme importance of a tolerant mind. In Harsha's time the general tendency was so eclectic that toleration of all creeds would have followed as a natural result even if Hindu tradition had pointed to the other direction. Harsha's ancestors were devout warshippers of Maheśwara, Aditya and other Hindu deities and Harsha himself, though he accepted the religion of the Buddhism, did not wholly give up the faith of his ancestors. No difference of religion even entered into considerations of State, and an orthodox Brahmin, like the poet Bāna, was as much the object of his favour and patronage as the pious Chinese pilgrim. His friend and ally Kumara Rajah of Kāmarupa was a convinced follower of Brahminism though he also imitated Harsha in extending toleration to men of all religions. The pious Master of the Law was himself invited and entertained by this king.

Of Harsha's charity and piety we have many instances. In the great assembly held at the city of Prayaga the king gave away to the poor and the needy all the wealth of his treasury. Indeed his charity seems to have gone to the extent of distributing the accumulated wealth of the State once every four years. Whatever we may say of this as a financial measure, there is no doubt that it was the outcome of a true spirit of charity for few are the kings who will loosen their purse strings except for pomp or glory. Like all pious kings Harsha built also a large number of temples, monasteries and other houses of religious worship. As a Buddhist for whom animal life was as sacred as human, he must have endowed large hospitals on the Asokan model and built rest-houses, dharmasalas (and other convenience) on the road.

Harsha has often been compared to Asoka; but there is no similarity between them except of the most superficial kind. The only point of comparison is perhaps that they were both patrons of Buddhism. But even here there is no similarity between the religious fervour and the missionary enthusiasm of Piyadasi and the latitudinarian eclecticism of Harsha. Asoka, after his conversion to the faith of the Buddha, spent his whole life for the propagation of the noble Dharma without in any way interfering with the beliefs of those who professed other forms of religion. For this purpose he worked day and night. Harsha, on the other hand, does not seem to have taken anything more than a dilettante's interest in the religious discussion of his court and never seriously set himself, except perhaps by liberal donations, to support the religion that he professed. A more suitable parallel than that of Asoka is Akbar. Like the great Mogul Emperor, Harsha extended toleraton to all, held religious discussions with the leading doctors of all creeds and was, like him, perfectly indifferent to the higher call of religion. Like the famous discussion in the Ibadat Khana, the disputations in Harsha's court never led to any result. Like Akbar, again, Harsha was a military monarch for the greater part of his reign.

In spite of obvious shortcomings Harsh was without doubt an enlightened monarch and deserves to be considered among India's greatest rulers.

Chapter IV.

THE SOCIAL CONDITION OF INDIA IN HARSHA'S TIME.

Of the condition of India under Harsha we perhaps know more that of any other period before the time of Al Beruni and the first Muslim conquest. The observant pen of Yuan Chwang has left us a picture, imperfect in many ways, but of such a kind as we have not in India before his time. His narrative is interesting and authentic, with a wealth of details in matters relating to social conditions and religious life. With the help of his descriptions supplemented by such evidence as can be gathered from the inscriptions of the 7th century, it is possible to reconstruct a picture of the social condition of India in Harsha's time.

The revival of Brahmininism which had taken place under the Gupta emperors and which contributed to the gradual, but none the less steady displacement of Buddhism was the great and outstanding religious fact of the 6th century. All the inscriptions that have been discovered show how firmly the predominance of Brahminism was established at the end of the Gupta period. The grandfather of Harsha himself was a firm upholder of *Varnasrama dharma* or Brahminical religion.[1] Yasodharman of Malwa was a worshipper of Siva as he himself declares in the Mandesor stone inscription. The founder of the Vallabhi dynasty was

1 Sonpat copper seal, C. I. I., Vol. III. p. 231.

a "most devout worshipper of Maheswara[1]". His descendents were mostly ardent followers of Hinduism, though Dhruvasena, Harsha's vassal and son-in-law, was reputed to be a Buddhist, more it may be presumed as a result of Harsha's persuasion than through belief. The kings of Karna Suvarna, we are distinctly told, were hostile to the creed of the Enlightened One,[2] and though Bhaskara of Kāmarupa patronised the learned Chinese pilgrim, he does not seem to have given up the religion of his ancestors to follow the Noble Eigth-fold Path. All along the line Brahminism had triumphed.

But it must not be thought that Buddhism had completely lost its hold on people in the 7th century. This was far from being the case. It is evident from Yuan Chwang's descriptions that the Buddhist Sangha or Order still possessed unquestioned sway over many millions in India. It should always be kept in mind that in no period of history had Buddhism monopolised state patronage or popular favour. Indeed, the view that is implied in the phrase 'Buddhist India' is an essentially false one. Except, perhaps, in the time of Asoka, Buddhism was never a state religion, and after his time as before Brahminism continued its sway over a great portion, probably over a majority of the population of India. But as Brahminism had no organised church, its influence was less obvious and perhaps less felt. With the beginning of the second

---

1 Maliya copper-plate inscription, C. I. I., p. 104.
2 Watters' Yuan Chwang's Travels, Vol. 1, p. 343.

century after Christ the vitality of the old Aryan-tradition again asserted itself and a gradual approximation between the two creeds took place. Thus was evolved the Mahayana form of Buddhism.

The simple creed of Gautama had, not long after his *Pari nirvana*, followed the inevitable course of all religions and became divided into a number of sects each claiming to be orthodox. The two main divisions were the Mahayana and the Hinayana, the greater and the lesser Vehicles. But these two sects were each again divided into many different schools. I-Tsing mentions 18 of them.

The difference between the Mahayana and Hinayana forms of Buddhism may be summarily stated here. The Hinayana doctrine was that Nirvana, by which was meant a total and absolute extinction can be attained only by contemplation (darsana) and meditation (bhavana) on the four noble truths. There were two main sects among them, called Pratyēka Budhdas and Srāvakas. The Hinayana led to a great emphasis on the formulæ of procedure. The Mahayana or the great Vehicle, which was a later development, was to some extent a devotional cult. The worship of the Buddhas was an important part of it. Its dogma was that in order to obtain deliverance from desire, ignorance and existence it is necessary to practise all the virtues and to acquire all the knowledge of the

---

1 La Vallee Poussin. Hasting's Encyclopædia. Art, Mahayana.

Buddhas.[1] From a philosophical point of view it was phenomenalist and its theology tended distinctly towards polytheism. Here, again, it was the influence of Hinduism that was at work. Two interesting developments of Mahayana Buddhism which strikingly evidence the same influence are the Tantrayana and the Mantrayana which are obviously forms of Vedantic Saivaitism in a Buddhist garb.

I-Tsing[1] gives us the names of 18 different sects of Buddhism. We must remember that the period of Harsha was not so much a period of Buddhist religion as of Buddhist scholasticism and hence the difference between these 18 sects was often based on some obscure point of psychology or formula. I-Tsing, though himself a theologian of learning, found it difficult to determine which of the 18 schools should be grouped with Mahayana and which with Hinayana.

Apart from these 18 sects 4 important philosophical schools had been developed in Buddhism by the middle of the 5th century after Christ. The Vaibhashikas and the Sautrantikas who may be called "realists" in our modern phraseology belonged to the Hinayana, while the Mahayana theory in philosophy was represented by two schools, the Yogāchāra and the Mādhyamika. The Mādhyamika school, which was the most influential, was founded by an Acharya named Nagarjuna. They were pure nihilists who held that

---

1 I-Tsing's Buddhist Religion in India p. 29.

the phenomenal world was illusory.[1] Here, again, we see Buddhist philosophy coming back to Upanishadic thought.

Of the state of Hinduism during the 7th century it is more difficult to speak. We pointed out before that Brahminism had always held its ground even in the days of Asoka and Kanishka. As a social order, Hinduism took its shape before the Buddha preached his creed. During historic times this order has changed comparatively little till our own days. What the Buddha protested against in the 6th century B.C. was almost the same organisation as Ram Mohan Roy protested against in the 19th. But if Hindu social organisation has shown an extraordinary immobility, the cults and creeds of the religion have changed with every century. Though the institutions remained the same, the beliefs and dogmas and the people underwent constant change. In the 7th century and the two centuries preceding it, Vaishnavism and Saivism had become dominant beliefs among the Brahminists. Harsha's own father was an ardent worshipper of Maheswara and the inscriptions of the 6th and the 7th centuries show that Siva worship was almost universal at the time. We know of the existence of this creed as early as the Christian Era[2]. Wema-Kadphises, a powerful prince of the Kushan dynasty (3rd century after Christ), claims to be a devotee of Maheswara, and

---

1 Sarva Darsana Samgraha, Cowell & Gough Pop. ed. pp.4-15.

2 Bhandarkar's Vaishnavism and Saivism. Grundriss der Indo-Arischen Philologie und Altertumskunde.

an image of Siva with the trident adorns the obverse of his coins. Kalidasa, even in his work on the dynasty of Raghu, which deals with Sri Rama, worships Siva at the beginning. Yuan Chwang mentions Pāsupatas (a sect of Saivites) 12 times in his book and we are distinctly told that these worshipped at the temples of Maheswara.

The predominant position of Saiva religion in the 7th century is also attested by the great rock-cut temples of Mahā mallapuram. Mahamalla Pallava was a contemporary of Harsha. Under him the Pallava power attained its zenith. The celebrated temples that he built to commemorate his glory were dedicated to Siva.

The rival cult of Vaishnavism seems to have been widely diffused, though not to the same extent as Saivism. This cult has been traced historically as far back as the 4th century B.C.[1] Its wide prevalence in centuries preceding Harsha's time is well-attested by inscriptions. The great emperors of the Gupta dynasty seem to have been Vaishnavites. Chandra Gupta II., at whose court Kalidasa flourished, styles himself Parama-bhāgavata on his coins. An inscription of Skanda Gupta tells us of a grant he made to a temple of Krishna. Some of the great Chalukya rulers were worshippers of Vishnu. Mangalesa, the uncle of Harsha's rival Pulikesin, had a temple erected for Vishnu to which, for the festival of dedication, he assigned the revenues

---

[1] Bhaṇḍarkar's Vaiṣhnavism and Saivism, p. 3.

of a village. In Bāna's *Harsha Charita* itself we have a mention of Bhagāvatas or worshippers of Vishnu. The rock-cut temples of Mahāmallapuram, though dedicated to Siva, have a number of monolithic granite sculptures of Vishnu as Lord of the World.

Apart from these two main cults, numerous other sects are known to have existed at that time. The description that Bāna gives for the representatives of different creeds who dwelt in the Vindhyas gives us a clear picture of the diversity of Hindu religious life. An interesting sect is that of the sun-worshippers. The inscriptions we have definitely proved the existence of a Mithraic cult. Harsha's own ancestors are spoken of as having been Paramādityabhaktās or devout worshippers of the sun. Frequent mention of kings who followed this religion shows that it was widespread. There is some evidence to show that this worship finally merged into the Vaishnava sect (witness the prevalence of such words as Surya Narayana.) The wide diffusion of heliolithic culture of which the main symbol is combination of the disc, the vulture and the serpent[1] and the importance attached to all these marks in Vaishnava mythology point to the same conclusion. The Chakra of Vishnu is certainly a representation of the sun. It is supposed to be self-luminous. Padma, the wife of Vishnu, is a synonym for lotus, the mythological consort of the sun. More than this, the Shank (conch) in Vishnu's hand is easily

1 Elliot Smith: Migration of Culture. Ryland, Library Memoirs. Manchester University Press.

recognisable as another element of the heliolithic or the sun-worshipping cult. It is, therefore, more probable than otherwise that the Pouranic deity of Vishnu is a complex of a number of religious cults and that his generous form has absorbed the worship of the sun which was then prevalent in India.

The actual religious life of India at that time was almost the same as it is to-day. The description that Bāna gives us of the life in Brahmin villages is not very far from prevailing conditions. Caste restrictions which form the basis of Hindu religious and social activity were as rigid then as they are now. Yuan Chwång, who was not able to understand them fully, made some curious mistakes in his description of the system, but that was only natural because no foreigner can understand the workings of such a complicated system in its entirety. More than this, the Chinese pilgrim was hardly interested in anything which was not Buddhist and his observations on Hindu India are cursory and not quite up to his usual standard. There is no dcubt whatever that the caste system as we know it to-day with all its elaborate restrictions with regard to marriage, food, ceremonial pollution, etc., existed in its fully developed form in the days of Harsha.

Education was very widely diffused in this period. We know that a great revival of learning took place under the Guptas which fcund its culmination in the splendid and unrivalled ccurt of Chandra Gupta II. The impetus of this movement seems to have lasted for another two centuries. We shall speak elsewhere about the literary glories of Harsha's reign. What is essential to remember here is that a wide diffusion of knowledge must certainly have been a prominent feature in the 5th, 6th and the 7th centuries in India. Perhaps, India of that time was the most educated country in the world. She was the academic centre of Asia whose universities eager students from China, Japan and the Far Eastern countries visited in a spirit of reverence. The Buddhist monks took great interest in education, and in all the Saṅghārāmas or monasteries there were adequate arrangements for the training of initiates and lay bretheren. Every important city contained many such Saṅghārāmas. We have Yuan Chwang's statement that in Kanauj alone there were some hundreds of Saṅghārāmas with some thousands of srāmanas. In Muttra, we are told that there were 2,000 brethren who were diligent students of both Vehicles. Every monastery was a college in which instruction was freely given in dialectics (Tarka), in Dharma sutra (Law) and in Buddhist scriptures. More than this, the novices were trained to live clean and honest lives.

Of all educational institutions in India at that time Nalanda was the greatest and the most celebrated. Of this noble institution we have a detailed description both in the life and in the travels of Yuan Chwang. The university was built and endowed by a local chieftain in the Magadha country by name Sakraditya. His descendents enlarged his gift and continued to patronise it. We are told by Yuan

Chwang that a long succession of kings continued the work of building, "using all the skill of the sculptor till the whole thing is truly marvellous to behold.[1]" It does not require any great gift of imagination to reconstruct in mind what marvels these colleges would have been architecturally. To students familiar with the remains of Buddhist art either in the form of massive structural work as at Boro Budur at Java or in the form of fresco painting such as have been preserved at Ajanta, Sigri and other subterranean monasteries, it is easy to realise what magnificent edifices would have housed the great university which was the pride of the Buddhist world.

The endowments of Nalanda brought it a princely income. Kings vied with each other in granting it villages rent free. In the 7th century,[2] it had the revenues of 200 villages, besides much other money in cash and other investments. The head of the institution was accorded royal privileges, such as are now enjoyed to some extent by the Sankaracharya of Sringeri Math and heads of other great religious houses.

Yuan Chwang gives the following description of the university.[3] "The students undergoing instruction " numbered several thousands. They are men of the " highest ability and talent. Their distinction is very " great at the present time. There are many hundreds " among them whose fame has rapidly spread through

---

1 Beal, Vol. II p. 170. 2 Beal, Vol. II p. 120. 3 Ibid.

" distant regions. Their conduct is pure and unblamable. They follow in sincerity the precepts of moral law. The rules of the convent are severe and all the priests are bound to observe them..... The day is not sufficient for asking and answering proposed questions. From morning till night they engage in discussion—the old and the young mutually helping one another. Learned men from different cities who desire to acquire renown in discussions come in hundreds to settle their doubts and then the streams of their wisdom spread far and wide. For this reason some people usurp the name (of Nalanda students) and going to and fro receive honour in consequence.... One must have studied deeply both old and new (books) before getting admission. Those students therefore, who come up here as strangers have to show their ability by hard discussion; those who fail compared with those who succeed, are as 7 or 8 to ten. With respect to those of conspicuous talent, solid learning, great ability, illustrious virtue, distinguished men, these connect (their high names) with the succession of celebrities belonging to the college, such as Dhamapāla and Chandrapāla who excited by their bequeathed teachings the thoughtless and the worldly. Gunamati and Stiramati, the streams of whose superior teachings spread abroad even now; Prabha Mitra with his clear discourses, Jinamitra with his exalted eloquence, Sīlabhadra and other eminent men whose names have been lost."

Yuan Chwang himself underwent a course of instruction in this university. At that time Sīlabhadra was the head of the institution. He was himself a disciple of Dhamapāla and Yuan Chwang always speaks of him with the greatest reverence and admiration. We are told how, when a young man of thirty, Sīlabhadra was selected by his Guru to go and hold public debate with heretic from Southern India who had challenged the scholars of the university. The distinguished Chinese pilgrim, whose fame had preceded him, was received by a deputation sent by Sīlabhadra and treated with becoming honour. There Yuan Chwang studied Yoga Sutras and many other Sastras with such diligence that he came to be regarded as one of the fifty most distinguished scholars of the university.

Though Nalanda was a Buddhist institution, the teaching there was not carried on in a sectarian spirit. We are told that among the subjects studied were included Vedas, grammar, logic, mathematics and medicine. All the different sects of Buddhism were represented and even Brahminical studies were not neglected. There can be no doubt that Nalanda was one of the greatest educational institutions that ever existed. In the 7th century it was unique in the world as being the only international educational centre. The enthusiasm of the Chinese scholar for his Alma Mater may have been coloured but the conscientious and upright monk and the careful and painstaking student whose whole life was one long record of perseverance in the cause of learning is certainly not the one to give anything but a strictly honest description of what he saw. In the case of Nalanda, especially, his testimony is one of the highest value as he himself was in residence in the university for a considerable period.

Of the condition of general education in the time of Harsha we have some details preserved to us in Yuan Chwang. The following is the description he gives us of the system of education then current :[1] "In beginning "the education of their children and winning them on to "progress they are taught a book of twelve chapters "(Siddha Vastu). When the children are of seven years "of age the five vidyas or sciences are gradually "communicated to them. The first science is grammar, "which teaches and explains words and classifies their "distinctions. The second is that of skilled professions "(concerned with) the principles of mechanical arts, the "science of causes (hētu vidya), and astrology. The "third is the science of medicine. The fourth is the "science of reasoning, by which the orthodox and the "heterodox and the true and the false are thoroughly "sought out. The fifth is the science of the internal "(Adhyatma vidya), which investigates and teaches the "five degrees of religious attainments and the subtle "doctrine of Karma."

The system evidently was a mixture of vocational and classical training. The earlier training was essentially secular and the children of ordinary men whether

1 Watters, Vol. I. pp. 154-55. Beal, Vol. II. pp. 78-79.

Buddhist or Brahminist went through a course of secular studies before they parted ways in higher metaphysics. The five vidyas enumerated before are most probably the course of Buddhist teaching, though it is probable that scholars among the Brahmins were also familiar with them as is evident from the fact that public disputations under royal patronage between the two schools were frequent and often continued for days together. It is certain that the most learned teachers of Nalanda and other Sangharāmas were proficient in all the different Sastras which were then current.

Higher instruction among those who followed Brahminical Hinduism followed a different course. The four Vedas were taught, evidently only to the Brahmins. The teachers were eminent scholars who had devoted their lifetime to the study of the various branches of knowledge. The method of teaching was meant more "to rouse the disciples to mental activity rather than to "instruct them in dogma. They instruct the innert and "sharpen the dull, and the teachers doggedly persevere "in giving instruction to those who are addicted to "idleness."[1] Unfortunately for us the pilgrim, who was more interested in the doctrines and teaching of Buddhism than in the method of Brahminical education, has given us only a meagre description of the course that Brahmin teachers followed. But considering the fact that when Yuan Chwang visited India Brahminism had almost regained its predominance in Arya Varta, it is certainly

---

1 Watters' Yuan Chwang's Travels p. 159. Beal, p. 78.

improbable that its educational organisation could have been in any way inferior to that of the Buddhists. It must also be remembered that the great intellectual awakening of the preceding two centuries was closely associated with the revival of Brahminical teachings.

Another factor of importance in the educational life of India at that time, as to some extent even to-day, is the influence of wandering monks and Sanyasins. Yuan Chwang was impressed by their wide learning and spirit of self-sacrifice. "Though their family be in "affluent circumstances, such men make up their minds "to be like the vagrants and wander here and there to "get their subsistence. Though they are not moved by "honour or reproach, their fame is far spread. Even "kings treated them with great respect. They were "deeply versed in antiquity and they devote their time "to the cultivation of knowledge."[1] Their influence on educational life must have been great for they wandered all over the country teaching poor students who were willing to learn.

Public religious disputations between famous teachers of various schools were very frequent. Eminent scholars from all parts of India travelled to great seats of learning, like Benares and Nalanda, to hold discussion with the advocates of other systems. In the century that followed Harsha's death we know that the great Sankara went to all the colleges and universities in order to propagate the truths of Advaita Vedanta,

1. Beal, Vol. II. p. 79. Watters, p. 160.

which he had elaborated. This was a very ancient custom in India, and was as common as knightly tournaments in feudal Europe. The discussion between the Buddhist patriarch Parsva and the Brahmin scholar Ashvaghosa which took place in the first century B.C.[1] is one of the most famous of its kind in Buddhist history. In the time of Chandra Gupta Vikramaditya of Ujjain, a great disputation between the exponents of the two rival religions was held on the subject of sense perceptions[2]. Manoratha, the champion of Buddhism, was worsted in the discussion owing to the Brahminical bias of the king. But in the next reign, Vasubandhu, the favourite disciple of Manoratha, won the victory for Buddhism and his master. The fame that followed a successful disputant in these assemblies was so great that it must have been an inducement to all scholars to persevere in their studies especially in the subtle theories of metaphysics and religion. This must have kept the standard of intellectual attainment very high among the theologians and professors of the universities and it must have reacted powerfully on the educational atmosphere of the country.

About the status of women in later Hindu times we have not much historical evidence to go by. Of the period immediately preceding Harsha's time the evidence afforded by literary works goes to show that women were held in high respect. Education was common among the women of the higher classes, and if we

---

1 Taranatha, p. 59. 2 Watters, p. 212.

may go by the indications afforded by Kalidasa's works now universally admitted to have been written in the Gupta period, it seems that a fairly high standard of literary culture was attained in feminine circles. Tradition tell us that Kalidasa's wife was herself a great literary personality who had vanquished many scholars in open debates, and we know as a fact that in the century after Harsha the learned wife of Mandana Misra adjudicated in the philosophical discussion between her husband and Sankara. Yuan Chwang tells us that Rajya Sri, the sister of Harsha, was present when he explained his doctrines to the king, and Bāna tells us that a famous Buddhist sage was engaged by the king to discourse to his sister on the Dharma.

Polygamy was not infrequent in the highest strata of the society. The Rajahs and the nobles had many wives, and it is probable that they were condemned to live in seclusion. But there certainly was no *purdah*, and we are definitely informed by Yuan Chwang that the Queen Mother of Baladitya expressed a desire to see Mihirakula when that Hun potentate was defeated and captured.[1] We are told that she was a princess of wide celebrity on account of her vigorous intellect. Marriage has, of course, always been a matter of religious necessity rather than of individual choice in India except in the case of Buddhist monks. A woman once married was not allowed to marry again. We shall not be far wrong if we suppose that in the matter of mar-

1 Beal, Vol. I. p. 169.

riage, widowhood, etc., the position has not altered to any great extent. Sati, or self-immolation, was not unknown but not common even among royal households. Queen Yasovati, the mother of Harsha, ascended the funeral pyre of her lord, and we are told in a Nepalese inscription that queen Rajyavati did the same on the death of her husband, Dharmadeva.[1] A Gupta inscription[2] mentions that when Gopa Raja was killed in battle, "his devoted, attached and beauteous wife accompanied him to the funeral pyre." Such instances must have been very rare for we have numerous mentions of queens who survived their husbands. We also know that Rajya Sri, in spite of the fact that she was a widow, was held in great esteem and even took her share in the administration of the realm.

The domestic life of the vast majority of the people in the 7th century did not differ materially from that of the Hindus of to-day. In fact, the theory of Hindu life has remained fixed from a much earlier date and the only development, if we except such protestant movements as that of Ramanuja and Nanak, has been in the way of rendering it more and more inelastic. The joint-family system, which is the peculiar feature of Indian life, was a well-developed institution even in the time of Harsha. With polygamy, enforced widowhood, and early marriage, Indian social life presented almost the same characteristics as to-day. Rajya Sri was married when she was a child. She was hardly 14 when she was left a widow.

---

1 Nepalese inscription No. 1. 2 C. I. I. p. 93.

Inter-caste or Anuloma marriages were common. Bāna, in discussing his ancestry, is careful to say that he was the son of Chitrabhanu, by a Brahmini named Rajadevi. He had two half-brothers, Chandra Sena and Mahi Sena through a Sudra step-mother. The marriage of the higher caste men with the women of the lower castes, as long as they were within the recognised *varnas* was not disallowed, though a Pratiloma intercourse, that is, association of lower caste men with higher caste women was strictly prohibited both by law and by religion.

The comparative quiet that the whole of India enjoyed during the first half of the 7th century must have led to a great development of trade. Maritime intercourse between Persia and the Chalukya kingdom, which is commemorated by a fresco painting in Ajanta, has already been alluded to. From time immemorial the west coast of India maintained relations with Egypt, Phœnicia, and other Mediterranean countries as is clearly proved by the wide prevalence of the various elements of heliolithic culture.[1] We are also told by the early travellers that the ports of the Arabian Sea coasts, chiefly Surat, Calicut, Cranganore and Quilon, carried on a brisk trade with all the known parts of the world. Fa Hian travelled by "a great merchant vessel" from Bengal to Ceylon. From Ceylon he sailed in another big merchantman which, we are told, carried two

---

1 See Prof. Elliot Smith, M.D., Migration of Culture. Ryland's Library Memoirs: Manchester Univ. Press, 1916.

hundred men. That such ships carried not only ordinary folk but even Brahmins is clear from Fa Hian's description of an attempt made by them to cast off the pilgrim "on any island they met," because to them it seemed clear that the storms that beset them in their voyage was due to his presence.

The 7th century was a period of intense colonial and maritime activity in India. The colonisation of Sumatra, Java and other islands of the Indian Archipelago was begun early in the first century after Christ, but it was when Harsha was the emperor of Northern India that the Saurastra emigration to Java[1] and Cambodia began. We are told that a ruler of Saurastra, forewarned of the coming destruction of his kingdom, started his son with 5,000 followers among whom were cultivators, artisans, warriors, physicians and courtiers in six large and hundred small vessels towards Java.[2]

The Bay of Bengal also saw some maritime activity. The Chola emperors of the next century were great navalists and maintained a powerful fleet. In the 7th century, Tamralipti was the great port on the east coast. I-Tsing, who followed Yuan Chwang, found it (as his two illustrious predecessors had found) a seaport town of great importance. It is now acknowledged that India in those days carried on an extensive trade with China, Japan and the islands of the Pacific.

---

[1] R. K. Mukherjee. A History of Indian Shipping.: Longmans p. 157. [2] Ibid.

About roads and land communications Yuan Chwang does not tell us much. The teachings of Indian political thinkers always emphasised the necessity of building good roads and planting banyan trees to give shelter. Sukraniti[1] lays it down that Raja-Margas, or king's highways, should be built for marketable commodities. Roads were to be constructed like the back of a tortoise (high in the middle) and were to be provided with bridges wherever required. It was a duty of prisoners to mend the roads with gravel. Rest-houses for men and beasts were to be constructed at stated intervals. That this was not merely the theory but also the practice can be seen from the fact mentioned by Yuan Chwang that Harsha built hospices provided with food and drink on all the highways throughout his dominions.[2] The very fact that the pilgrim was able to move about freely all over India shows that the roads were kept up in good condition. The frequent progress of the king up and down the country, of which Yuan Chwang has given us a good picture[3], necessitated the building and upkeep of roads in an excellent condition. Where there was no bridge, ferries were provided and a light duty was imposed for their use.[4]

That these roads were comparatively safe may be inferred from the fact that the pilgrim was able to go

---

1 Sukra Niti, pp. 34-35.

2 Beal, p. 214. It is interesting to note that until very recent times this tradition was kept in the two Hindu states of Travancore and Cochin.

3 Beal, p. 215. 4 Watters, p. 176.

unattended from one end of the country to the other. The existence of feudatory Rajahs everywhere with civil and criminal jurisdiction must have tended to greater safety. But it would be a great mistake to presume that the efficient police organisation of the 20th century existed in those days. Highways must have had their dangers then, but they could not have been very great as we know definitely that there were swarms of Bhikshus and Sanyasins moving about the country. A police force was maintained. We have the mention of *Chaurodhararikas* (literally the catchers of thiefs) or officials entrusted with the extermination of thiefs,[1] and often in records of grants fines on villages for harbouring thiefs are alluded to.

Agriculture was then, as now, the chief source of India's wealth. India was perhaps the best irrigated country at that time, records showing that even in the time of Mauryas, kings took great pains to have canals dug and dams constructed.

Artisans and craftsmen were organised in guilds. Of the presence of trade guilds in ancient India we have sufficient evidence.[2] The Indore copper-plate inscription of Skanda Gupta (A.D. 456) specially mentions the guild of oilmen residing at Indrapura, to whom land was assigned as a perpetual gift, to be enjoyd as long as they continued to be in complete unity.[3] Says the grant:

---

[1] Watters, 178 [2] R. K. Mukherjee's Local Government in Ancient India. Oxford. 2nd ed. p. 36 et seq. [3] Ibid. p. 71 ch. II vol. III.

"The gift is the perpetual property of the guild of " oilmen of which Jivanta is the head residing at this "Indrapura as long as it continues in complete unity." We have also an inscription dealing with a grant to a guild of silk-weavers at Dasapura. The guild held property in common, meted out justice among its members and enjoyd other privileges of a body corporate.[1] Bāna, in describing the scenes of Rajya Sri's marriage, mentions the guilds of leather workers, carpenters and plasterers.[2]

In Harsha's time the towns of India perhaps presented the same outward aspect as typical Indian cities do now. Yuan Chwang's description would certainly suit any Indian city of to-day as much as that of the 7th century. He says—"the streets and lanes are tortuous and the roads are winding. The thoroughfares are dirty and are arranged on both sides of the road with appropriate signs."[3] Certain classes of people such as scavengers, butchers, dancers and executioners were not allowed to live within the walls. They were allowed only on the left side of the road when they entered the municipal limits. As to how the town affairs were managed Yuan Chwang does not tell us. We know, however, from a Gupta inscription that an official called Drangika existed in every city. He probably exercised the functions of a mayor and he was assisted

1 See Mukherjee's Local Government, with regard to the Privileges of Guilds. Chaps. IV., V. & VII.

C. & T., 123 & 124. 3 Beal, Vol. II. p. 78.

by Mahattaras (literally elders) who were probably councillors representing the inhabitants. As we know that the affairs of the village were managed by a Panchayat, it is reasonable to believe that towns also enjoyed such a privilege and that authority in the town was vested in some popular authority.

The chief town in India at that time was Kanyakubja, the capital of Harsha. Pataliputra was in ruins, though it must have been imposing even in that condition. Mathura was an important Buddhist city with about 20 Sanghārāmas. Benares, the centre of Hindu India, has been, at least from the time of the Buddha, a city of great sacredness. "They were mostly unbelievers there ; only a few reverence the Law," so deplores the pious pilgrim.[1] There were in the city a great many Deva temples, the towers and halls of which were of sculptured stone and carved wood. Ujjain, though perhaps its glory had departed with the decline of the Gupta empire, was still a university town of great renown where astronomy seems to have been the speciality. From casual allusions in Yuan Chwang we know that there were many other cities where learning was prized and facilities for both education and economic enterprise existed. But no description of their size, population or industries is available as Yuan Chwang is very sparing in details when he is not dealing with miracles and bodhisatwas.

---

1 Beal, Vol II p. 73.

The chief city in the south was Kanchi, the seat of the great Pallava monarchs. The town, as it exists to-day, attest to its greatness in times past. Under the Pallavas it was one of the most magnificent towns of India, and a popular Sanskrit ditty says that as Kalidasa is the greatest of poets and the Ganges the most sacred rivers, so Kanchi is the most beautiful of all cities. Vatapi or Badami of Pulikesin II was a city which rivalled Kanauj and Kanchi till Nara Simha Mahamalla, the Pallava conqueror, razed it to the ground when he conquered it in 640 A.D.

Of the condition of art and architecture in the time of Harsha the direct evidence afforded by monuments is very little. There is not, I believe, any single architectural remains of buildings known to have been built by Harsha himself. Yuan Chwang tells us that the Viharas of the Buddhists were buildings of great beauty, and that they were constructed with extraordinary skill. The doors, windows and the low walls are painted profusely. The monks' cells are ornamental on the inside and plain on the outside. But not a single work of the time has survived in Northern India.

That Harsha's reign was a period of great activity and achievement in arts and architecture is evident from the fact that some of the best fresco paintings of the caves of Ajanta were executed in the time of Pulikesin, Harsha's great rival. It is during the same period that Nara Simha Pallava built the great cave temples of Mahămallapuram. The fine painting of Buddha with a blue lotus in his hand in Ajanta was a work of this period. It is very unlikely that when such a great creative impulse was manifesting itself over half the peninsula, in the courts of the two other monarchs who shared with him the sway of India, that Harsha, who was a great patron of art and letters, was behind his rivals in the matter of building great and noble edifices. In fact, Bāna mentions more than once that a group of skilled painters painted auspicious scenes.[1] The iconoclastic zeal of the early Mahomedan invaders has left us not even a trace of these highly valuable things. Kanauj, Harsha's capital, is now an unimportant town. Nothing is left of the many magnificent structures by which the great emperor of North India adorned his capital or showed his piety.

---

1 C. & T., p. 124.

CHAPTER V.

HARSHA—THE POET.

THE golden age of classic Sanskrit was the fifth, the sixth and the seventh centuries after Christ. The growing ascendancy of Brahmanism brought in its train a great literary awakening which added to the lustre of the Gupta dynasty. Even the political anarchy that followed the breaking up of that empire consequent to the invasion of the Huns did not materially affect the growth of Sanskrit literature. The reign of Harsha witnessed another outburst of literary production second only to the period of Chandra Gupta Vikramaditya. Harsha himself was a great poet and dramatist and his court contained many eminent men of whom the chief were Bāna, Mayura and Bhartrihari.

Harsha was the author of three dramas, Naganandam, Priyadarsika and Ratnavali. Unfortunately, the question of Harsha's authorship has been a matter of great, and as we propose to show, ill-informed controversy.

That the three dramas were composed by a powerful king of the name of Harsha is evident from the texts.[1] The first question that arises then is that whether the Sri Harsha who, according to the prologues, wrote these dramas was the same Harsha Siladitya of

---

1 Raja Sri Harsha devasya padapadmopajivina raja samuhenokta: asmat svamina, Sri Harsha devena purvavastu racana lankrta Priya darsika, &c. This description is seen in all the three dramas.

the line of Pushpabhuti whose achievements Banâ commemorates. History knows of five other persons who bore the name of Harsha. The first is the half-mad tyrant of Kashmir who ruled that State from 1089-1101.[1] The second is Sri Harsha, the grandfather of King Bhoja of Dharanagar. The third is that elusive personality, Vikramaditya Harsha of Ujjain,[1] at whose court Matragupta lived.[2] The fourth and the fifth Harshas—the authors of Naishadhīya carita and Kavya pradipa—respectively were not kings at all and therefore can be dismissed from the controversy. Of the Harshas who were monarchs and for whom claims of authorship have been advanced, the one who was the chief of Dharanagar and the grandfather of Bhoja can be proved to have lived in the earlier half of the 10th century from the fact that his son Munjaraja, the paternal uncle of Bhoja, lived in the later half of that century. That this Harsha could not have written the dramas in question is clear from the fact that Damodâra Gupta in his work named Kuttini mata, which is a production of the 8th century A.C., gives us the story of Ratnavali and quotes the 24th sloka of the first act and praises the play as a work of great beauty. This Damodara Gupta was a minister of Jayapida[3] who ruled Kashmir at the end of the 8th century. It is thus impossible that a king who lived in the 10th century could have been the author of a work which was known widely and quoted with eulogistic

1 Stein, Rajatarangini, p. 357.

2 Stein, Rajatarangini. p. 83.

3 Ibid. p. 116 & Peterson's Introduction to Sabhashita Ratnvali.

commentary in the text of a kavya known to have been written in the 8th century.

The same argument rules out the claim put forward for Sri Harsha of Kashmir. Even otherwise that tyrant, who is accused by Kalhana[1] in more than once place as a Turuska or a Mahomedan and is described by the same authority as the embodiment of all that is immoral, could never have been the author of the Buddhist play Nagananda. But all such considerations apart from the question of time alone places him out of the controversy.

The claim put forward for Sri Vikramaditya Harsha of Ujjain is more serious and demands more detailed examination. Rajatarangini of Kalhana which incidentally describes the achievements of this king is significantly silent about his learning but merely says that he betook himself a poet called Matragupta.[2] More than this, we are expressly told that Harsha was only his secondary name while the title he took was that of Vikramaditya. Yuan Chwang also mentions him only by that time. The author of the plays is uniformly spoken of as Harsha and it is certainly unlikely that a highly prized title like that of Vikramaditya would have been consistently left out if the author possessed that name also.

All these arguments have only been negative. Before we proceed to show that Harsha Vardhana was himself the author of these plays it is necessary to refute a statement based on hearsay which has found currency

---

1 Rajatarangini, pp 353 & 357. 2 Ibid. p. 83.

among critics and scholars. It is said—as we propose to show on very spurious authority—that the author of these plays was really the great Bhāsa, who is sometimes, here again wrongly, identified with Dhāvaka. Bhāsa was till recently a mysterious personality in Sanskrit literature. He was known chiefly by the appreciative allusion of Kalidasa in one of his prologues and till the curator of the Trivandrum Sanskrit Library series discovered and published them, his writings were considered to have been completely lost. It is said that these three dramas were written by Bhāsa who sold them to his patron for a consideration of money. This theory is based on a statement in Raja Sēkhara's Sārngadhara Paddhati which says that Bhāsa wrote Priya darsika and the other dramas and sold them to Sri Harsha Vikrama who made its author a poet of his court.[1]

The absolute impossibility of this would be evident to any one who reads the works of Bhāsa which have, fortunately for Sanskrit literature, now been recovered. Literary evidence would also prove that the three plays are much later in point of time than Kalidasa's and two of them are in fact modelled upon that author's Malavikāgnimitra.

Another theory based on equally unreliable evidence is one to which currency was given by the commentary

---

1 Adau bhasēna racitā natikā priya darsikā nirigasya rasanjasya, kasya na priya darsana Tasya ratnāvali nūnam, ratna mālēva rājetē Naganandam samā lokya, yasya Sri Harsha Vikrama Amandānandā bhr ita, swasabhyāmākarot kavim.

of Nagoji Bhatta on Kavya Prakasa. The commentary itself merely says that it is possible (by being a poet) to earn fame like Kalidasa and money like Dhāvaka. There is nothing either in the passage or in the commentary that justified the elaborate stricture of Nagoji Bhatta. Nagoji, a very late commentator leaving both the original and the earlier commentaries behind, explained the passage by saying that it is possible to earn money as Dhāvaka did by selling the authorship of his works to Harsha. This statement has certainly no value in as far as it was written nearly 1000 years afterwards and based entirely on hearsay.

As to Harsha Siladitya's own claim we have more or less definite proofs. Bāna distinctly says that Harsha was a great poet.[1] He is stated to have taken part in dramatic performances. More than this, Nagananda is a Buddhist play and none of the Harshas we know was a Buddhist. I-Tsing also definitely says that Siladitya versified the history of Jimuta Vahana who sacrificed himself for a Naga. Harsha Vikramaditya was an orthodox Brahaminist. Again, Madhusudana, the editor of Mayara Sataka, in his commentary called Bhāvabodhini, specifically says that the king in whose court Bāna and his brother-in-law Mayura lived was the author of the three dramas. That Harsha Siladitya would have bought the works of other authors in order to plume himself as a great author is contrary to known and notorious facts with regard to his character. We can,

---

1 C. & T. p. 86. Rajatarangini, p. 83.

therefore, be reasonably certain that Harsha wrote these plays in spite of what critics may say.

Of these three dramas Ratnavali and Priyadarsika are plays relating to fashionable society in which the plot centres round the intrigues of the court. They are very obviously modelled on Malavikagnimitra. The story in both Ratnavali and Priyadarsi is very much alike and quite simple. Indeed, both of them are quite in the conventional style. The king falls in love with one of the maids of honour to his queen who reciprocates his love. The inevitable Vidúshaka, or jester, is used as the go-between by the parties. The queen gets to know of the intrigue and attempts to thwart the passion of the king but later on finds that her maid of honour is a high born lady entitled to share the affections of her royal husband. This satisfies her honour and every thing ends well by the marriage of the hero and the heroine.

In the present case the hero of both Ratnāvali and Priyadarsika is one king Vatsa of Kausambhi. King Vatsa is a hero of many romantic tales and his amours form the favourite theme of Hindu romancers. It is quite probable that, as in the case of Agnimitra, there is a historical basis for Harsha's dramas But whether there is or not, they are illustrative of the court life of the time and the impression that one gains by a study of the plays in this aspect is that at least in the higher social circle a very high degree of refinement was attained. From the purely artistic point of view it cannot be said that either Ratnavali or Priyadarsika have anything distinctive in them to entitle its royal author to a considerable place in Indian literature. The lyrical quality of the verses in them are of a very high order and this alone perhaps constitutes their merit to be classed among minor classics of India.

Nagānanda is a work of an entirely different kind. Here Harsha does not follow the mere conventionalities of dramatic art. The story itself is interesting. Jīmutavahana while searching for a hermitage in the Malaya hills, sees the daughter of a king of the Siddhas. He falls in love with her, though she is a yogini devoted to the worship of Parvati, the Consort of Siva. She tells him of a dream that she had in which the goddess appeared and made known to her that the king of the Vidyadharas will become her husband. Malayavati also falls in love with Jīmutavahana and they are parted without each knowing the identity of the other. Mitravasu, the brother of Malayavati, offers her in marriage to Jīmutavahana, but ignorant of the fact that she is the object of his love he refuses her hand, and Malayavati knowing this, determines to commit suicide. The cries raised by her companion bring Jīmutavahana to the spot and the misunderstanding is cleared up and they are married with great festivities. In the meantime the hero is informed that his kingdom has been seized, but realizing that his high dignity will only mar his happiness, Jīmutavahana refuses to proceed against the usurper,

So far neither the story nor the treatment has anything distinct or peculiar about it. The hero falls in love with a princess practising devotion in a hermitage, and this is a common theme in Hindu drama. If the play had ended with the third act it would be a drama of the conventional style, only comparatively feeble and uninteresting but still a complete play. But in Nagananda the action does not begin till the 4th act. Jīmutavahana after his marriage while walking with Mitravasu came across a heap of skeletons. His brother-in-law explained to him that the remains were those of serpents who were offered up daily to Garuda, the king of the birds and the mortal foe of serpents. Jīmutavahana was greatly shocked at this and, taking pity on the cries of a mother whose son was to be offered to Garuda that day, approached her. But the old woman mistaking the hero for Garuda offered to die in the place of her son. His natural sense of pity was now reinforced by this touching scene and Jīmutavahana offered to substitute himself for the young Naga. Though the Naga refused to take advantage of this Jīmutavahana went up to the place of sacrifice while the mother and the son went to pray in Siva's temple. While he was thus offering himself up to Garuda, his own father, Malayavati, and others came out searching for him, troubled by the fact that one of the gems of the crown of Jīmutavahana was seen falling. The young Naga, in whose stead Jīmutavahana had offered himself as sacrifice, was able to find the bird and he prayed that he himself may be eaten and the prince spared. But alas, it was too late. The bird had eaten him already. The remains of Jīmutavahana are cremated and his wife and other relations follow him to the pyre. This terrible act of sacrifice affects even the heart of Garuda and feeling remorse for his horrible demand absolves the serpent-king from the treaty. The dead Jīmutavahana is recalled to life, however, by the intervention of the goddess Gauri who had promised Malayavati that her husband would be the king of the Vidadharas, and in order to fulfil this Jīmutavahana is reinstated in the throne of his fathers. Thus the story ends happily.

This story differs obviously from the general run of Indian dramas. The only other work in Sanskrit dramatic literature which may be said to belong to the same genre is *Uttara Rama carita* or the later history of Rama by Bhavabhuti. But even here the comparison is only superficial. In both the central theme is pathos. In a carita *Uttara Rama carita* the poet's theme is the agony of separation (Viraha) while in Nagananda it is the profound sense of pity that moves us. Harsha in his treatment of the story displays a singular power of description and narration. The scenes are vivid and in some places they reach the very height of tragedy.

Harsha's position in Indian literature can hardly be said to be with the highest. Ancient Indian criticism placed him high—

> Yasyā corāscikura nikarāh karna pūrō Mayūrō
> Bhāsō hāsah kavi kula guruh Kalidāso vilāsah
> Harsō harsō hrdayavasatih pancabānastu Bānah
> Kēsam naisā kathaya kavitā kamini kautukēya.

In this verse Jayadeva, the author of Gita Govinda (the Indian Song of Songs), appraised his eminent predecessors. Cora is the mass of locks, Mayura is the ornament of the ear, Bhāsa is the smile, and Kalidasa, the master of all poets, is the charm, Harsa is pleasure, and Bana is the five-arrowed cupid. How could the damsel of poetry then be other than charming.

Modern critics of Sanskrit literature will hardly give so high a place to Harsha. As a dramatist he does not possess either the unique charm of Kalidasa or the dignity and beauty of Bhavabhūti. His two court plays do not rise to anything above the level of pretty farces. Nagananda is certainly a dramatic piece of great power but its poetic quality does not entitle its author to a very high place in literature.

Harsha was also a great patron of letters. Of all the writers who adorned his court the best known is Bāna, the author of Kadambari and Harsa Carita. He is acknowledged to be the greatest romancer in Sanskrit. His Harsa Carita together with Hari Sena's life of Samudra Gupta and Kalhana's Rajatarangini form the best known trio of historic compositions in Sanskrit. The two important works of Bāna—Kadambari and Harsa Carita—are both prose works. They are written in a style which is highly artificial and hardly differing from poetry except in the fact they are not metrical

That he was a writer of extraordinary ingenuity with an unrivalled command of words and a marvellous imagery no one will doubt. But his method of description is so ornate and his sentences so involved that his pre-eminence acknowledged by all pandits will not so easily be granted these days. Indeed the orthodox view places Bāna very high in the ranks of Sanskrit poets. *Bānōscistam jagat sarvam*—the world of poetry is merely the leavings of Bana. Very few will now be found to subscribe to this exaggerated estimate.

With all his faults it must, however, be admitted that Bāna is among the immortals of Sanskrit literature. Kādambari in spite of its over-decoration is a well-told romance which will always be read and appreciated by Sanskrit scholars. The ubiquitous use of *Slesa*, which makes any translation into English impossible, is not a mere exhibition of pedantry which it seems to be to a foreigner, but a highly interesting and enjoyable form of poetic expression to which there is no equal in European languages. In Harsa Carita also this *Slesa* style is beautifully worked out as, for example, in the famous passage in which Harsa's greatness is described as superior to that of every king known to ancient history.

Bāna's brother-in-law, Mayura, was also a celebrated poet. Of his works only three have come down to us.

(1) Surya Sataka, a century of verses in praise of the sun.[1]

---

[1] This has been published with a commentary in the Kavyamala series.

(2) Arya Muktamala, of which a copy is known to exist in a private library at Surat.[1]

(3) Mayurastaka, or the eight verses of Mayura.

According to a persistent and universal tradition in India, Mayura became afflicted with leprosy. It is said that he was cured of it as a result of his worship of the sun-god for which purpose he wrote his Surya Sataka. It is still a belief in India that leprosy can be cured by worshipping the sun according to certain ancient rites.

The great poet Bhartrihari also lived in Harsha's time.[2] It does not seem, however, that he was actually at Harsha's court. This great poet is perhaps the most widely read of all Sanskrit writers except Kalidasa. He is said to have thrice given up the world to follow the Noble Eighth-fold Path but each time he returned to the pleasures of lay life. Of his poems it is unnecessary to speak as they are some of the best known in the whole range of Sanskrit literature.

Of the literary history of the period only one point more need be mentioned. The development of Prakrit as a literary dialect seems to have proceeded apace during this century. Among Bāna's friends there was a Bhasha or vernacular poet. The beginnings of literary Hindi are perhaps traceable to this distant period.

---

1 Buhler's Catalogue of Sanskrit MSS. in Gujerat, 2nd Vol., p. 72. 2 I-Tsing p. 60.

CONCLUSION.

FROM the foregoing sketch it should be clear that India, in the first half of the 7th century had reached a comparatively unique state of civilisation. In Europe at that time forces of anarchy and barbarism had completely destroyed the civilisation of Rome. Persia was in its last stage of degeneration in which it fell an easy prey in a few decades to the onslaught of Muslim invaders. In China, the great and glorious dynasty of the Tangs ascended the throne only in 618. The Celestial Empire was at that time very much under the influence of the creed of the Buddha. To the Chinese of the time India was the sacred land. Traversing deserts and mountain ranges her children visited India in a spirit of veneration in order to study at her univesities and partake of her culture. It is undeniable that India in the 7th century was the most civilised country in the world.

The reign of Harsha may thus be said to mark the culmination of Hindu culture. From the next century the period of decline may be said to begin. In literature, in art and in education the later ages showed no development. The decadent classicism of the Maha Kavyas and Champūs of the 8th and the 9th centuries is typical of the decay of sciences and letters that followed the break-up of the last great empire of Northern India. It is Harsha's glory to have been the last in the long line of Hindu rulers beginning with Chandra Gupta Maurya in whose time India appeared to the world not only as an ancient and mighty civilisation, but an organised and powerful State working for the progress of humanity. There is no doubt that Harsha, the ruler, the poet, and the religious enthusiast will ever have an honoured place in Indian history.

MATERIAL AVAILABLE FOR A STUDY OF HARSHA'S LIFE.

THE two primary authorities for the life and times of Harsha are the *Harsha Carita* of Bāna and the travels of Yuan Chwang. Though Bāna's *Harsha Carita* has been known to scholars for long, its historical value was not fully recognised till Yuan Chwang's travels were translated from Chinese and published. Now it is admitted on all hands that Bana's poem is a work of historical merit of great value and rare accuracy. Bāna's prose, as we have noticed elsewhere, was highly artificial and complicated and hardly suited to a historical composition. In fact, his idea was certainly not to write a biography but a kavya glorifying the achievements of his patron. In doing so he mentions the facts of his life. His attempt is to make Harsha appear like one of the kings whose greatness is celebrated in the Puranas. In a classic passage he wants to show that Harsha is even greater than all his predecessors. He is compared to all the gods and fulsome praise is bestowed on him.

The value of *Harsha Carita* does not depend entirely on its historical accuracy. As a picture of social and political life of an ascertained age it is of the highest importance. His own early life and training that Bāna describes is as important to us as the campaign of Harsha to recover Rajyasri. Here even his elaborate descriptions come to be of value. His detailed narration of the court as he saw it though fantastic and exaggerated to a degree shows us the nature of royal camps as they continued to be down to the very days of British occupation.

Though fantastic in many respects Bāna never allowed his imagination to carry him away from historical facts. This is best exemplified in his description of Harsha's ancestry. He makes no attempt to connect his patron with any mythical god or hero. The fabrication of ancestry is a pleasant and to some extent a harmless pastime of all biographers. But Bāna's statements in this matter have been borne out by the sober researches of history.

Unfortunately, Bāna's romance deals only with the early history of Harsha. The period of Harsha's political activity is left untouched by Bāna. But here we are supplied with the full and copious memoirs of the illustrious Chinese pilgrim Yuan Chwang. Yuan Chwang was no ordinary pilgrim. The Tripitaka Master of the great Compassion Monastery was a sage and scholar who was held in high esteem in his own country. He was descended from an illustrious family which traced its descent from the Royal line itself. Yuan showed early in his life a thirst for knowledge and an enthusiasm for Buddhist learning which made him desirous of visiting the native land of the Divine Master. But such an undertaking was no easy job. But Yuan undertook it with courage and was fortunate enough to meet with no serious accident on the way.

He stayed in India for 15 years and his travels extended all over the country. Unlike his predecessor Fa Hian, Yuan Chwang had a keen eye for observation. His book of travels entitled *Si yu ki* is a classic in Buddhist countries. It throws a flood of light on the social and political conditions of India. It is true that in matters connected with Buddhist miracles Yuan was easy of belief almost to the point of credulity. But it must be remembered that he was essentially a pilgrim with a perfect and unbounded faith in the religion of the master. But this does not take away the value of his observations on the political and social state of India. He was on terms of intimacy with Harsha and his vassal kings and went all over India as a royal guru.

His narrative differs profoundly in style from the romance of Harsha. The simple matter-of-fact descriptions of the Chinese pilgrim bear strong contrast to the high-flown and ornate style of the poet. But the picture of the country which these works present is found to be in singular agreement. Bāna though he ends abruptly by about A.D. 629 and Yuan though he does not begin till about A.D. 630, corroborate and supplement each other. The value of both of these works does not lie in their being works of history. They are descriptive more of social conditions than of purely historical facts. It is as such that their value has to be estimated.

Harsha Carita has been translated into English for the Royal Asiatic Society by Cowell and Thomas. The translation is done with extraordinary skill and ingenuity and is a model for all such work. Yuan Chwang's work is available in English through the translation of Beal "Buddhist Records of the Western World" (Trübner & Co., London, 1888). It has been rendered into English also by Thomas Watters (Vol. XIV and XV of the books published by the Oriental Translation Fund.) The rendering is critical and the notes are extremely valuable.

There has been so far only one published life of Harsha. M. Ettinghansen's "Harsha Vardhana: empereur et poet" (Paris, 1906) brings together all the material then available. Unfortunately, it is more imaginary than otherwise and the utilisation of the material has not been very satisfactory.

Of the other material available for the period under study much lies buried in the volumes V to VIII of *Epigraphica Indica* and the back numbers of the *Indian Antiquary*. Fleet's Gupta inscriptions—C. I. I. Vol. III—is of course the most important primary source of our archæological evidence. It is the groundwork of all study on Indian history during our period. Dr. Indraji's inscriptions from Nepal is invaluable for matters connected with that kingdom and Stein's translation of Rajatarangini has been found very useful in many important matters. I-Tsing's Record of the Buddhist Religion in India translated by Takakusu (Oxford, 1896) is of value in studying the religious problems of the time.

Of the secondary authorities Vincent Smith's "Early History of India" is easily the most important. It describes Harsha's career in detail and utilises with great skill all the material available. For the history of the Deccan and Southern India I have depended mostly on Sir Ramakrishna Bhandarkar's classical "Peep into the Early History of the Deccan" first published in the *Bombay Gazetteer.* Prof. Jeaveau Dubreuil's "Ancient History of the Daccan" is a well-documented, scholarly work dealing with a period that is insufficiently known. The same author's work on the Pallavas has also been found very useful. Other books are acknowledged in the footnotes.

FINIS.